Words

I lost bend my finger in a horizon and words, birds of words, hop on it, chirping.

Words

_{I but bend my finger in a beckon and words, birds of words, hop on it, chirping.}

By Bob Brown

A Facsimile

Edited and with an Introduction by Craig Saper

Cataloging-in-Publication Data is available at the Library of Congress

2014940402

First published Bob Brown, Roving Eye Press, 1930
First published by Roving Eye Press, 2014

Roving Eye Press
www.rovingeyepress.com
RovingEyePress@gmail.com

Introduction: For Words © Craig J. Saper, 2014
All rights reserved

Book Design by Deborah Fay

ISBN: 0-692-21725-8
ISBN13: 978-0-692-21725-2

Printed and bound in the United States of America

Contents

Introduction: For Words by Craig Saper	vii
Works Cited and Further Reading	xxi
A Note on the Text	xxiii
Words	1

For Words
by Craig Saper

For Words

In the reading-machine future
Say by 1950
All magnum opuses
Will be etched on the
Heads of pins
Not retched into
Three volume classics
By pin heads.
    —*Bob Brown*

In January 1931, Bob Brown worked with Nancy Cunard's Hours Press to publish *Words*—two sets of poems printed in a single volume. The book was subtitled *I but bend my finger in a beckon and words, birds of words, hop on it, chirping*. One set of poems was printed in 16-point Caslon Old Face, a classic font style used in all Hours Press publications. The other was relief-printed from engraved plates at less than 3-point size (perhaps, according to Cunard, less than 1-point). Because the subtitle was also printed in the microscopic text, archives, libraries, and bibliographies often mistakenly omit it.

Although Brown was, for Cunard, "at the very center of his time, a *zeitgeist* in himself," they printed only 150 copies, and the book passed into relative obscurity. It is generally mentioned only as a footnote in discussions of Cunard's life or in reference to *Readies for Bob Brown's Machine*, Brown's better-known anthology of experimental texts by modernist writers, including Cunard herself (Cunard, *Hours*, 177 and 181).

One can place *Words* at the intersection of three lineages. Nancy Cunard wanted to produce elegant modernist works in the fine-press artists' book tradition that Hours Press helped initiate: "to achieve impeccably clean things with fingers grease-laden" (*Hours*, 9). Brown wanted to demonstrate how microscopic texts for his reading machine might appear if printed next to poems set in 16-point type. A reading of the book from the perspective of an avant-garde audience places it in the tradition of art-stunts. (In this regard, Brown's friends, George Antheil and Marcel Duchamp, influenced his interest in art-stunts involving machines and mechanisms.) As a performance of reading strategies, *Words*, with

Introduction

its magnifying glasses and hidden clues, alludes to detective stories or to the paranoid's micrographia and *art brut*.

Only a handful of scholars have had the opportunity to read *Words*, which this new edition makes widely available, and even fewer have discussed it outside of a passing mention or footnote (for exceptions, see Dworkin, 2003, or Ford, 1988). The current moment seems ripe for a rediscovery of this work precisely because of contemporary interests in book arts, reading technologies, conceptual art projects, and interdisciplinary modernist studies.

Nancy Cunard, famous for her iconic glamorous fashion with African bangles and bobbed hair-style, was part of a thriving group of small-press publishers in the 1920s, including Contact Editions, Beaumont Press, Ovid Press, Nonesuch Press, Fanfrolico, Seizin, Sylvia Beach's Shakespeare & Company, Black Sun Press, Black Manikin Press, and Bob Brown's own Roving Eye Press. She announced *Words* in a December 1929 edition of *transition*, the English-language modernist art and literary journal published in Paris. She started talking about the possibility of the project after Brown had sent her a copy of his " beautifully produced" *1450-1950*. The title refers to the evolution of printing, and its meaning was immediately clear to Cunard, a printer; but the poet William Carlos Williams wrote to Brown wondering what the "numerals meant" (*Hours*, 177; Williams, n.p.).

Cunard saw in Brown's work "another new slant" in the ongoing experiments in reshaping writing by the surrealists, Dadaists, and others (*Hours*, 177). The design and craft involved in its production make Cunard and her printers more collaborators than simply invisible technicians. Clearly, Cunard embraced the "pristine joie-de-vivre" of the "persistent experimenter" looking for "felicitous discoveries." She and Brown both were "intoxicated by words," yet knew "how to bring them to heel" (*Hours*, 178). Both shared passions for ethnography, collecting, and—most of all—work. Their intense productivity, with Brown publishing five of his books and Cunard's press producing ten books in 1930 alone, speaks to an atmosphere of expatriate excitement for writing and publishing.

The story of Brown's collaboration with Cunard is, to borrow Hugh Ford's phrases, the "story of how books were made, of how ideas became the words on a printed page," and of how "author and publisher conferred during each step of the production of the book." The lesson that this edition of *Words* should teach us is that small presses "could and did cultivate an intimacy between authors and publishers as well as a creative atmosphere that large commercial publishing houses, now as well as then, nearly always lack" (Ford, *Hours*, xv-xvi).

Unfortunately, many literary accounts of the twenties and thirties focus on the personal lives and fashions of artists rather than their work, except to dismiss it all as symptomatic of the scene's decadence. To Hugh Ford, the historian of these expatriate publishers, books like *Words* demonstrate "the solid literary achievements of people who for too long, have been either dismissed or glorified, depending on the classifier, as a 'Lost Generation'" (Ford, *Hours*, xv). Brown describes the situation in an untitled poem on page 19 of this volume: "But for years I have / Peered through venetian blinds / At poets / Without yet catching a glimpse of / One at work." Indeed, we might know more about what they drank (Brown, for example: beer and wine, not whiskey), and who they had affairs with during the late 1920s and early 1930s than about what they accomplished. Many summaries of Nancy Cunard's life prominently feature her affairs with the co-founder of surrealism, Louis Aragon, or the co-founder of Dada, Tristan Tzara, or the African-American jazz musician Henry Crowder. One appendix to a biography includes a lurid tale about George Moore, the influential poet and novelist, who repeatedly asked Cunard to let him see her naked (Cunard, quoted by Fielding, 188-9).

Biographical summaries recount all these love affairs with important men but few details about the processes and pleasures of the work both Brown and Cunard loved: the "love of printed letters" (Cunard, *Hours*, 183).

In relation to the self-reflexive poetry about the work and pleasures of printing, both Brown and Cunard had intense, even erotic, connections to their work. Cunard named Hours Press as an allusion to the work and work habits of her friend Virginia Woolf, who, with her husband Leonard, gave Nancy advice about the endeavor she was about to undertake; the Woolfs knew from their Hogarth Press that "Your hands will always be covered in ink." The process of printing and writing are rarely the motif of poetry, but for Cunard, "the smell of printer's ink pleased me greatly, as did the beautiful freshness of the glistening pigment. There is no other black or red like it. After a rinse in petrol and a good scrub with soap and hot water, my fingers again became perfectly presentable;

the right thumb, however, began to acquire a slight ingrain of gray, due to the leaden composition" (*Hours*, 9). They were "looking at possibilities, at possibilities say, of bringing innovations up against some of the consecrated rules of layout" (*Hours*, 10), which for them had become a kind of prohibition.

Brown's work in publishing and printing and voluminous writing made one line of the opening poem in *Words* a coda of his life: "words and I are one." He also includes a visual mathematic formula as part of the poem, suggesting a quantifiable and scientific description of the merger of poet and words rather than a mawkish metaphor of two people merging in love.

Cunard always printed in the serif Caslon Old Face type on the heavy Vergé de Rives paper, both of which she acquired in "generous amount" when she purchased a 200-year–old hand-press from Bill Bird, whose Three Mountain Press had already published modernist poets Ezra Pound, Ernest Hemingway, William Carlos Williams, and others (Ford, *Hours*, xii). With her press, inks, paper and type, Cunard quickly established a look for all of the books she published, and she also commissioned covers by Louis Aragon, Paul Eluard, Georges Sadoul, Man Ray, Yves Tanguy, Elliott Seabrooke, and Len Lye.

Brown's project would throw a wrench into that tidy process and house style. Although Cunard had hoped to design the binding for *Words* as "a reproduction of a large slab of old ivory, the veining standing out dark on the printed surface, this turned out to be too difficult; the reproduction would not have been sharp enough. So the covers are cream paper boards with a red leather spine" (*Hours*, 182). The cover design by John Sibthorpe, perhaps the only element that went off as planned, resembles a typewriter poem from the 1950s and 1960s rather than a modernist printing exercise.

No one involved in the project ever thought to give the book's miniature font a name, since it was a one-off, not produced as moveable type and never used again. The microscopic text might be categorized as an illustration of printed letters or a visual poem about microscopic printing rather than a traditional font or typeface. It seems appropriate, in the context of this reissue of *Words*, to name this font "Bobbed Brown Condensed," after Gertrude Stein's appellation "Bobbed Brown"—her witty allusion to Brown's call in his *Readies* manifesto to process all texts in a telegraphic cut-up style eliminating all unnecessary words.

The microscopic text, "too small to be read without a magnifying glass" or without using a variant of Brown's proposed reading machine, "strained the ingenuity and perseverance" of the Press's management when they sought type small enough for the micrographic poems (Ford, *Published in Paris*, 286). The "only solution, a costly one, was to print the miniature poems from specially engraved plates, the whole to measure not more than one-eighth of an inch when completed" (*Published in Paris*, 287). For Cunard, the project served as "an excellent example of what one plans to do and how circumstances can alter the idea. Many attempts were made to get really microscopic type" (*Published in Paris*, 183). The originally planned heavy paper stock would not work with the microscopic text that tended to blur as it imprinted in the rougher paper; they substituted a different, smoother, paper stock called Canson-Montgolfier to get a crisp, rather than luxurious, print. The efforts to engrave the copper plates and relief-print the text produced mixed results, with many letters either appearing— even with magnification—as dots, smudges, or typed over.

In Stein's aforementioned allusion, "authors bobbed sentences like a flapper's popular hairstyle: cut short" (Saper, *The Adventures of Bob Brown*, 66). Cunard refers to her own readies contribution as "condensed" (*Hours*, 181), and Brown certainly thought much about mass-produced condensed products since he would, in the 1930s and 1940s, co-author many cookbooks with his wife and mother. In *Words*, the type is "cut short" in an entirely different way: instead of with dashes as in *The Readies*, it is reduced with microscopic scale. In reference to this cutting-short process, Brown writes in the opening poem, "Operating on words -gilding and gelding them / In a rather special laboratory equipped with / Micro and with scope." Both sets of poems, 16-point and micro, perform a semi-autobiographical illumination of the literary and cultural meanings of printing in both form and content. For Cunard, the poems express the "Bob Brown spirit" and dynamism: "Everything about him had zest" (*Hours*, 184, 180). The content of the poems often employs an Imagist style to telescope concrete luminous details, like the image of hollow dice, into abstractions about (in the case of the dice) the lessons of Pandora's box and, in general, about art, printing, reading, and life.

The experience of reading *Words* suggests, in parodic fashion, the miniaturizing of secret messages by spies. (A century after *Words*, the U.S. government fends off counterfeiters' efforts by using "micro-printing" techniques to produce micrographic lettering; it's the same strategy Brown used for poetic ends.) Common in actual espionage and military intelligence, the trope of secret messages was a staple of pulp stories. In the first decade of the twentieth century, Brown wrote for the pulps using many pseudonyms—his own version of a secret identity. His most famous and popular story, made into the first serial movie, included episodes with secret messages, intercepted letters, and interpretations of message fragments.

During the early months of World War I, Allen Norton, a friend of Brown's, was arrested in Liverpool with a bundle of experimental poems and writings because the authorities thought he was "carrying dangerous messages that were clearly written in code" (Brown, *Letters of Gertrude Stein*, 1). Brown's first conception of a reading machine, also in that same year, took the code machines of the time as a type of readymade and as a way to avoid censorship even as the microscopic or processed *readies* would inevitably attract the censors' bemused attention. In that sense, the machine highlighted the emerging peculiar ways of reading abbreviated code systems: you have to change your pace and focus. We find this abbreviated language in stock market tickertape, shorthand, technical manuals, recipes, and specialized actuarial and accounting codes that came into widespread use in the first quarter of the twentieth century.

The microscopic poems in *Words*, initially planned as smaller versions of the otherwise identical larger poems, became separate works for technical reasons (the publisher could not fit the longer poems in the miniature space). So instead of the reader choosing whether to read the same poem in different sizes, and making the actual reading of the miniature poems a merely imaginative activity, the technical problems led to a different experience in which the poems seem to comment on each other.

For example, the poem "TO A WILD MONTANA MARE" portrays a sex scene in 16-point font for all to read. On the same page, hiding in what looks like a thumbprint or smudge, is a miniature poem about the narrator's lack of Romantic awe when visiting cultural icons like the Sphinx. Printing the sex scene in 16-point type next to the poem about great cultural wonders of the world in microscopic type pokes fun at censors' arbitrary choices: Why not censor a poem about the lack of appropriate passion and excitement during pilgrimages to the Sphinx, Leonardo's *Mona*

Lisa, and Michelangelo's Dome? Brown uses the unique design (the combination of micro- and 16-point fonts on the same page), and the anticipation of a reader's reactions, for poetic effect.

Brown continued his deconstruction of censorship in his volume *Gems*, which he printed and published in the same year as *Words* and dedicated to Cunard in the hope that she would find in it a "lifelong fountain of innocent and exalted pleasure" (Brown, *Gems*, n.p.). He also begins that collection of found poems with a detailed discussion of Havelock Ellis, whom Cunard also published, and whose books on sexuality were banned, denounced, and burned in England. With this ongoing prohibition in mind, Brown thought of his use of micrographic texts strategically, not ornamentally or neutrally.

The short filler form of the micro-poems was not new to Brown, who plundered his own popular-culture past to produce an avant-garde literature, a kind of pop-vanguard. It was essentially a genre—the "squib"—that launched his career more than two decades earlier. His first series of publications in 1907 consisted entirely of squibs, similar to the found-joke–like mistakes from other publications placed at the bottom of a column in the *New Yorker*. In one of his newspaper columns, he published jokes about signs one might see on the street, funny ads one might read in the town's paper, or simply comically odd sights in the city: "an up-and-coming clothes cleaner's sign reads, 'We'll dye for you'"; others that caught his eye (or ear) included "Grinn & Barret, Plumbers," and "Farswego: the name of every streetcar terminal according to the conductor's unintelligible, 'Far as we go.'" His column, which promoted "Foolsophy," also used this short form in parodic aphorisms: "A man is driven to both drink and suicide —he walks to work"; "A tack in the hand is worth two in the foot."

One can read visual-social-semantic poetics, or what I call elsewhere "sociopoetics," in the micrographic poems. In one such poem, titled "Zany Zed's Inarticulate Skeleton," the alliterative play, the repetition of letters, the capitalization of the alliterating letters, and the allusion to articulated skeletons poetically hint that the visual form and layout (or articulated skeletons) remain mute except in this "zany" comic bit.

In another (untitled) micro-poem (the micro-poems often have no space for a title), the word play involves Louis XV using the bilingual visual pun on Louis *quinze* (fifteen) as Louis quince (which works visually but not homophonically). One squib pokes fun at British food. Another describes red type on white paper. One describes the natural cynicism of a newspaper man when dealing with words, much like a baker distrusting a pie or a butcher looking at tripe. (Brown saw himself as a newspaper publisher who needed to fill column space with squibs and who distrusted writing with an editor's eye.) Another micro-poem wonders about the relation of thought to type on the page, and yet another complains comically about writing with a fountain pen (using the image as a way to consider the larger issue of writing technologies). The mini-poem "Death of Words" suggests a textual script for a comic book or movie treatment by using all capitals to indicate loud sounds, and em-dashes to suggest a shorthand system much like the system used in the *Readies* anthology, with its cinemovietone quality. The condensed poems, packed in a small space like the condensed soups that soared in popularity in the 1920s, provide an analogy for the post-book reading experience, with variable magnifications and focus.

In the condensed poem "New York 1930," Brown again illustrates the analogous relationships with other technologies, like cranking Ford cars (a favorite theme of Gertrude Stein's), talkies, telephones, vending machines, audio plugs, phonographs, and the experience of watching a movie of a Rhino braying when someone twists its tail and cranks the camera (perhaps an allusion to *Simba*, released in 1928, one of the first nature documentaries). The poem uses a staccato style suggesting a series of similar images (wires, cranks) and activities (jiggling, twisting, turning) to produce a new type of cinemovietone poetry.

Changing the focus (literally) to the larger poems, one sees the same satirical intent and a similar focus on printing, reading and writing, through titles like "Lament of an Etcher," "A Grace Before Writing," "Writing," "Sonnet (count the lines)," "I But Bend My Finger In A Beckon and Words Birds of Words Hop on it Chirping" (the poem's title as well as the subtitle of the collection), and an homage to Harry Crosby, the printer-poet. Brown later proposed using the image of the bent finger as part of an animated introduction to his plans for a "poetry TV" series, which was rejected by his agent and never proposed to any network or production company. The finger would bend and the animated words would jump on it and hop around like birds chirping (Brown, "letter," 1951).

There is a multicultural perspective throughout these poems. One, republished in his aptly named *Nomadness*, personifies Nirganth, a Persian meditation toward a detached sensibility. Brown also makes fun of European national figures, customs and mores, as in a poem about street dogs in the upscale spa town of Royat, in France. One untitled poem expresses a goal of the volume: "In the reading-machine future / Say by 1950 / All magnum opuses / Will be etched on the / Heads of pins / Not retched into / Three volume classics / By pin heads." The opening poem of the collection, about birds of words, is a poetic explication of the process of deflating the long-winded into congealed, condensed constructions.

In this volume, Brown does not give us the sort of clever neologism for his nanowritings that he offered when he coined the term *readies* to describe processed texts for machinic-reading. Brown sought in *Words* to demonstrate the processes involved in his planned reading machine; perhaps it was a more accurate demonstration than the anthology of readies for Brown's machine published the year before. Around forty years old when he lived and worked as an expatriate poet-publisher (with his Roving Eye Press in Cagnes-sur-Mer), Brown had already packed many other careers and millions of published words into the years before meeting Cunard. He saw this project as an explicit part of a campaign to announce his reading machine, and he published this volume not as an artists' book but as a demonstration of text preparation suggesting the future mechanics of reading.

The poems allude, in form and content, to the ways his life inflected his peculiar plans for the machine. Brown also worked in publishing and printing magazines, reading the tickertape as a stock trader, writing more than a thousand hugely popular stories for the pulps (where he sometimes worked for H. L. Mencken), book dealing, traveling the world collecting artifacts and learning about cuisine (for the many cookbooks he published after his expatriate years), and writing advertising copy. He had written Imagist and visual poetry since the early teens of the twentieth century, and knew many artists and writers from a decade before in Greenwich Village and the Grantwood artists' colony in the Palisades, New Jersey.

Opening up *Words* suggests an alternative (untaken) path for word processing and conceptual poetry. When the last line of the first page repeats that other theme of Brown's work, "words and I are one," it suggests also that the reading machine and Brown are one. Brown did in fact sometimes describe himself, with his amazing productivity, as a reading and writing machine, collecting books, reading everything he could get his hands on, and cranking out publications. Brown saw himself and words imbricated one upon the other, with his oystering eyes glued to the page.

Flipping through the book, one might find a poem that focuses on the need for a new poetry more attuned with the technologies of speed than is traditional poetry. In one such poem, Brown announces that "cloddish earthen poetry feet," with the pun on feet suggesting metrical units stuck in the mud, await a change in word production and distribution analogous to the airplane's impact on travel. Although not a new idea, since the Futurists had begun exploring it more fully twenty years before, and even advertising had explored the notion, Brown sought to enter a conversation about the teaching of reading and how mainstream culture published texts.

The effort to conceive and print *Words* produced poetry demanding a technological solution just to read it; it thus put reading at a further remove from a natural human activity (i.e., you cannot simply read this text, nor can you look at it as art design without meaning). In order for the reader to see the smudge at the bottom corner of the page as a microscopic poem, he or she needs an external apparatus (a machine either as simple as a magnifying glass or as complicated as a computer). The human eye has no zoom function. Where *The Readies* emphasized the linear motion on the x-axis, *Words* focuses on the z-axis. Imagine a machine that supersedes the un-aided human eye with scanning and magnification in constant change and motion; this volume presents a print-version simulation, where you toggle between large and small texts.

Reference to the history of micrographic writing, neither explicit nor exact in *Words*, begins at least by the time of Cicero, who reportedly saw an example of it. By the seventeenth century, it had been used in printing. In terms of using microscopic text to avoid censors, *Micrographia* (Hooke, 1665; new edition edited by Ford, 1998) discusses miniature writing and its possible utility in sending secret messages. Microfilm was used in libraries before the turn of the twentieth century. The surrealists' interest in miniature writing arose with reference to Jean-Martin Charcot, an influence on Freud, discussing micrographia as a symptom of neurological disorders at the close of the nineteenth century. Miniature books and book collecting were popular around the turn of the century as well. In banking and business, microfilm became more than a novelty or secret in the late 1920s, and those uses inspired Brown. His microscopic print alludes as much to condensed foods as to the precise history of graphic design, and his conception of the history of microscopic printing and writing was filtered through his own adventure-story imagination rather than through a scholar's erudition.

Keeping open the question of Brown's intent, whether the emulation of a business practice or the production of a Duchampian provocation (Brown having been influenced by Duchamp since 1912), clearly the experiments in reading suggest mechanical or artificial alternatives to the school-taught reading practices in the twentieth century. Before the school reform movement of the 1920s, school primers focused on small literary gems for recitation (Ravitch, 253). Brown takes aim at the censors' purported goal of protecting school-age children from less exalted literary works (like limericks, which seem especially suited to recitation and rote memorization). Mainstream forms of concise writing styles (e.g., text messages, scrolling stock quotes, fine print on products and contracts, etc.) resemble visual poetry more than composition primers. Outside of typography and graphic design, students are not taught the poetics and semantics of font size. When we say "read the fine print," we mean read the content, not the form or tone. In school, we do not teach how to read the fineness (the super-condensed smallness) of these ubiquitous forms of writing.

Brown makes explicit the scientific seriousness of his project. In his descriptions of his machine, he talks about his "recondite research" and "actual laboratory tests" (Brown, *The Readies for Bob Brown's Machine*, 4, 5). Describing the technical specifications of his machine, he compares it to commercially viable reading machines of the day rather than avant-garde stunts or provocations. What looked like avant-garde art and poetry in *Words* looks in *The Readies* like a scientific demonstration of the hyper-concise writing now sent out wirelessly, in reader-decided font sizes, as txt: MEGO ;-) (translation: my eyes glaze over <wink>). Brown would have loved this abbreviated form. He might have written the miniature poems in txt, delivered the poems on an e-reader, and made the small squares of text function like picture-in-picture replicas of the larger poems (as he intended).

Words, then, speculates on the future of reading and references the history of printing.

These descriptions of his intentions and research process speak to the mundane reality of early twenty-first–century media technologies. Interactivity, new formats that do not depend on multiple lines of print, the ability to change and control font size and how fast the text moves, and a shift toward visual (rather than phonetic) texts all seem familiar in the context of twenty-first–century reading and writing technologies. Brown's work could easily serve as the prophetic description of a newfangled software program that seeks to make reading user-friendly (more portable, in a smaller package, served up wirelessly, hyper-fast, and linked with instantaneous access to larger libraries of information). This potential software would free text, once "bottled up in books," to deliver variable-focus works for use on a PDA (Brown, *The Readies for Bob Brown's Machine*, 30). This practical program would teach the user how to switch from phonocentric reading (sounding out each word) to visual reading (changing lens and magnification). Perhaps Brown would be producing infomercials for his nano-poem machine if he lived during the turn of the twenty-first century rather than the turn of the twentieth. There are precedents, after all, for literary and artistic vanguardists to become inventors. George Antheil, the self-proclaimed enfant-Futurist, composer and performer of cacophonous mechanized concerts, and friend of Bob Brown's, invented, with Hedy Lamar, a spread-spectrum system for torpedoes that did not find a popular outlet until recently, when cellular telephony employed it. Moreover, the avant-garde was fascinated with markets, as Duchamp demonstrated when he tried to sell his optical art-toys like a street vendor in front of prestigious art exhibits.

Texts for reading machines appear both in *The Readies* and in *Words*. What would the machine look like that was made for texts like *Words*? The struggle to print *Words* brings on the dream of a machine (a typewriter or electronic device) that could produce microscopic texts. Although some might convincingly argue that the modernist effort to explore vision and work as separate from personality might have ultimately failed (see, for example, North), Brown dreamt of a machine that would remove vision and reading from one individual's perspective. This nano-reading machine would make the reader's eyes figuratively pop out of his head and, to borrow the title of Brown's first visual poem, float away like "Eyes on the Half Shell" (Brown, *Blindman*, 3). Whether an impeccable example of a modernist artists' book, an apt analogy for the experience of machine-enhanced reading, or a captivating surrealist art-stunt, *Words* deserves to find an audience beyond the fewer than 150 vanguardists who got copies in 1931, or the few contemporary scholars reading it in an archive today. We may now be ready to see what was hidden in the fine print of *Words*, and learn to refocus our eyes on the future of reading as revealed by what once seemed a mere novelty, an avant-garde artwork, a clever joke.

Works Cited and Further Reading

Brown, Robert Carlton. "Eyes on the Half Shell," *Blindman*, No. 2, New York, May 1917: 3.

Brown, Bob (aka Robert Carlton Brown). *1450-1950*. 1 ed. Paris: [Roger Lescaret for Harry and Caresse's] Black Sun Press, 1929. Reissued, New York: [Jonathan William's] Jargon Books, 1959.

---. "Letter to Bertha Case" (dated September, 1951): n.p.

---. "Letters of Gertrude Stein." *Berkeley: a journal of modern culture*, No. 8, 1951: 1-2, 8.

---. *The Readies*. 1 ed. Bad Ems: [Bob Brown's] Roving Eye Press, 1930.

---. *Readies for Bob Brown's Machine*. Cagnes-sur-Mer: [Bob Brown's] Roving Eye Press, 1931. BBM in text.

---. *Words: I but Bend My Finger in a Beckon and Words, Birds of Words, Hop on It, Chirping*. 1st ed: [Nancy Cunard's] Hours Press, 1931.

---. Gems. Cagnes-sur-Mer: [Bob Brown's] Roving Eye Press, 1931.

---. *Nomadness*. New York: Dodd, Mead & Company, 1931.

Cunard, Nancy. *Negro Anthology*. Ed. Nancy Cunard. London,: Published by Nancy Cunard at Wishart & co., 1934. New Edition, *Negro; an Anthology*. Ed. Nancy Cunard and Hugh D. Ford. New York,: F. Ungar Pub. Co., 1970. Re-issued, New York: Continuum, 1996.

---. *These Were the Hours: Memories of My Hours Press, Reanville and Paris, 1928-1931*. Edited with a Foreword by Hugh Ford. Carbondale, IL: Southern Illinois University Press, 1969. Referred to in text as "Cunard, *Hours*."

Dworkin, Craig. *Reading the Illegible*. Evanston, IL: Northwestern University Press, 2003.

Fielding, Daphne. *Those Remarkable Cunards: Emerald and Nancy*. 1st American ed. New York: Atheneum, 1968.

Ford, Hugh D. *Published in Paris: A Literary Chronicle of Paris in the 1920s and 1930s*. 1st Collier Books ed. New York: Collier Books, 1988.

---. "Foreword." in *These Were the Hours: Memories of My Hours Press, Reanville and Paris, 1928-1931*. Edited with a Foreword by Hugh Ford. Carbondale, IL: Southern Illinois University Press, 1969. Referred to in text as "Ford, *Hours*."

Hooke, Robert, and Brian J. Ford. *Micrographia* [London, 1665]. Facsimile edition in the Octavo digital rare books series. Palo Alto, CA: Octavo, 1998.

Huddleston, Sisley. *Back to Montparnasse, Glimpses of Broadway in Bohemia*. Philadelphia, London: J.B. Lippincott Company, 1931.

North, Michael. *Camera Works: Photography and the Twentieth-Century Word*. Oxford ; New York: Oxford University Press, 2005.

Ravitch, Diane. *Left Back: A Century of Failed School Reforms*. New York: Simon & Schuster, 2000.

Saper, Craig. "The Adventures of Bob Brown and His Reading Machine: Abbreviated Texts 50 Years Before txt, Twitter, and WWW." *The Readies*. Ed. Craig Saper. Rice University Press, 2009.

Stein, Gertrude. *Absolutely Bob Brown, or Bobbed Brown* (unpublished). Printed by Claude Fredericks at The Banyan Press in Pawlet, Vermont, 1955. Gertrude Stein and Alice B. Toklas Collection, Yale Collection of American Literature, Beinecke Rare Book and Manuscript Library.

Williams, William Carlos. [unpublished letter], dated Sept. 12, 1929, to Brown. Box 108, Bob Brown papers, 1844-1960, Collection #723, Special Collections, Young (Charles E.) Research Library, University of California, Los Angeles. Accessed by Paul Stevens on July 22, 2009. The relevant quote reads "Many thanks for the poems "1450-1950" tho' what the numerals indicate I haven't been able to make out."

A Note on the Text

The poetry set in microtext was studied by six pairs of eyes over three years: those of the editor of this volume, a series editor, the Rice University Press editor-in-chief, an archivist, a photographer, and a twelve-year-old with excellent eyesight. Final determination was based on the copy held at the University of Virginia's Special Collections, but other copies were consulted. The microtext reproduced here was reset because scanning technology could not properly reproduce the original printing, largely due to age-delivered deterioration of the original microtext. The editorial intent is to deliver the reader experience Brown intended, which was to compose microtext that is readable with the aid of a magnifying glass. In almost all cases, we were able to reproduce Bob Brown's text as it appears in the original. In the case of one line, which proved indecipherable to everyone consulted, we have reproduced the digital scan of the original. The struggles that the initial printers had with this text, as described in the afterword to this volume, were paralleled in our production process.

— Craig Saper

```
W     W    W    WORDSW     WORDSW    WORDSW     WORDS
O    OO    O    O      O   O     O   O     O    O
R    R R   R    R      R   RDSWOR    R     R    RDSWOR
D    D D   D    D      D   D     D   D     D    D
S     S    S    SWORDSS    S         S     SWORDS    WORDS
```

BY

```
bobrown   bobrown   bobrown        bobrown   bobrown   bobrown    bb   bb   b    b    b
bo   b    b    b    bo   b         bo   b    bo   b    b    b     or   r or  r    r bb  r
bobrown   o    o    bobrown        bobrown   bobrown   o    o     bo o bo o  o oo  o
bo   b    b    b    bo   b         bo   b    bo   b    b    b     w w  w w   w bb  w
bobrown   bobrown   bobrown        bobrown   bo   b    bobrown    n    n    n    n
```

```
           words
          bobrown
         wordswords
        wordsbobrown
       wordswordswords
      bobrownbobrownbob
     wordswordswordswords
      bobrownbobrownbob
       wordswordswords
        wordsbobrown
         wordswords
          bobrown
           words
```

```
h    h   hoursh   h    h    hoursp   hours       hours       hoursp   hours    hours    hours
o    o   o       o    o    r         h           o    p      o        r        h        h
upressu  u       u    u    upresse   hours       upress      upresse  upress   hours    hours
r    r   r       r    r    r         s           p           r        r        s        r       p    p
s    s   spresss rpresss   s    s    hours       s           s        s        spress   hours    hours
```

```
p    p   paris    p    p    p    p    p    p    p
a    i   a        a v  e a    a    a    a    a
r    e   r        r    i r    .r   .r   .r   .r
is   is  isvie    is   is     ss ix ss ix ss ix is
```

Words

I but bend my finger in a beckon and words, birds of words, hop on it, chirping.

by

BOB BROWN

HOURS PRESS

15, *Rue Guénégaud PARIS*

1931

TO
MY ROSE-RIB

150 COPIES OF THIS BOOK
SET BY HAND AND PRIVATELY
PRINTED ON HAND-PRESS
EACH COPY HAS BEEN
SIGNED BY THE AUTHOR

THIS IS NO

Bob Brown

I BUT BEND MY FINGER IN A BECKON AND WORDS BIRDS OF WORDS HOP ON IT CHIRPING

Operating on words — gilding and gelding them
In a rather special laboratory equipped with
Micro and with scope — I anesthetize
Pompous, prolix, sesquipedalian, Johnsonian
Inflations like *Infundibuliform*
Only to discover by giving them a swift
Poke in the bladder they instantly inspissate
And whortle down the loud-writing funnel.
Experimentally pricking with a sterilized needle
The centipedantic adjective *Pseudepigraphous*
I find it just goes Puff! and guiltily seeks
Sanctuary behind the dictionary.
All clearly classical words fray easily
The wooliest ones show undeniable traces of
Mouthy cotton. Weevil words bore.
Altiloquential ones when dropped in the
Specimen jar brimming with alcohol
Die torturously unhappy deaths from drowning
While wassail words run around the slippery rim
Making whoopee, shouting for a ducking
Coming out aglow to slip their warm little
Hands in mine with quaint curtsies from the
Lady ones and hearty "Thanks for the drink,
Old man," from their cheery red-cheeked mates
'Tis then I reach for the Laboratory Record and
Happily indite a new-found formula
          WW -|- I = 1
      (Words and I are one)

ILLUMINATION

Nirganth, Persian Princess
Petal of Spring
Vermillion-tipped
Jewelled fingers and toes
In the golden grass
Of the Garden of Love
Singing the
Soul Song of Spring
To her swan-headed zither

Widowed *Nirganth*
Burdened with black baubels
On the flower-lit bank of the
Brook of Spring
Her sobbed song
Attracting full-mated, tail-tossing
Goats and ducks
And curious, timorous virginal things
With tails between their legs

Nirganth stands
Stark, alone and straight
As the stately, solemn fruitless palm
Behind her
Between two full-branched bearing trees
And two others with
Main limbs lopped off

Nirganth, widowed
Greets seminal Spring
With ritual
Sighing her plaintive
Autumnal dirge
Mid cavorting, inquisitive goats

TO A WILD MONTANA MARE

Lady Godiva
Why
Did you keep me
Awake all night
Last night
Tossing
Lifting white-hot sheets
On my perpendicular tent-pole
A lonely maverick
Making camp in the
Desert of my bed
Gazing through
Gossamer gloom
For glowing glimpses of
Your dimpled
Blank-faced
White Bottom
You siren centaur
Clattering night mare
In the cobbled street
Below my scholarly garret

I am no
Lime-washed
Out-washed
Jet black stallion
To be whinnied at
Neighed at
Nipped
By the vicious mind of a
Flare-eyed
China-toothed
Nipple-dappled
Wide-flanked
Back-biting
Heel-tossing
Hell-fire
Explosive
Back-firing
Pinto pony
Wild-maned
Montana Mare
Like you

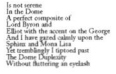
Is not serene
In the Dome
A perfect composite of
Lord Byron said
Eliot with the accent on the George
And I have gazed calmly upon the
Sphinx and Mona Lisa
Yet tremblingly I tiptoed past
The Dome Duplicity
Without fluttering an eyelash

THE PASSION PLAY AT ROYAT

There is no great gulf between the
Love life of the
Dogs in the village street of Royat and
Other dogs or even human beings
Only a subtle distinguishing finesse of
Full-blooded frank expression.
With Royat dogs spring is always here
Hope lurks forever
Just around the next lamp-post
They bark and bite, snarl and scratch
Purr and piddle, play ceaselessly at
Fornicopulation
Even as talkie actors in gilt ritzyrooms.
But the dogs of Royat never think of
Pulling the shades down or the sheets up
Openly in public they purify their bodies
Fornify themselves happily
Against the rigours of a cold world
Grinning with dripping red jaws
Wagging lively laughing tails
Enacting the commonly recurrent functional
Momentary crises of existence
Out in the middle of the street
All day long industriously rehearsing their
Realistic Passion Play in public

Looking down a little on their peers
Saintly solemn Oberammergauers and other
Formal puffed-up pallid passion players
Who, like barnyard roosters
Piously await the
Peal of the Angelus
Before paying their
Pompous duty calls

ARMED HOSPITALITY

Down haunted horridors
Asceptic nurslings wriggle
Balancing bed-pans
Brandishing hastily-snatched
Baby pink catherters
Burying their blazing cheeks in the
Public dirty-clothes bag
Hiding behind lavatory doors
To lure into hot pursuit
Scalpel-eyed satyric internes
Practicing interment

With one obsidian brow
Lifted for the Main Chance
And the other
Well up the Main Hatch
Assisting at Caesareans
Making vermiform appendixes squirm
Helping stitch up livid belly seams
Forgetting surgical scissors inside.
Clanging through town in helmets
Astride brass-lunged ambulances
Courageously picturesque
Volunteer Out-snuffers of The Eternal Fire

Poking probing fingers into
All too human apertures
Bringing yowling Babes
Rosebuddy and blistered
Into this drab dripping Wood
Turning them up to impulsively
Talcum their mucilaginous mucosities
Daintily dabbing the bawling bastards
With demi-rouge compacts
Inadvertently slipped from
Viscous concealment by
Nuzzly Leda-necked goosey nurslings
In their paroxysmal
Spasmodic scurrying
Down haunted horridors

HARRY CROSBY

Freshly-new, mentally-lithe
Sound, cleanly-sane
Sportsman in Life
Eager modern art experimenter
Rimbaud reincarnate
Pioneer in the Infinite
Fourth dimensional venturer
Harry Crosby discovered
The Ultimate Pole
Located neither North nor South
First nor last, here nor there

As a human projectile
Self-shot into the
Blinding black centre of his Sun
Crosby's grey ashes were not
Scattered alone over Manhatton
But flashed for a full
Millimetre-second
In a bursting rainbow meteor
Trailing resplendent sparks
A scintillating shower of
Formulated Futurity
Glowing radiantly through
Time-Space from hopeful
Realms of Rising Suns to
Earthy haunted sad-eyed Setting Suns,

And mole-eyed mousey people
Squinted up at the spectacle
Clutching for their Faith
Frantically in miraculous reticules

Brilliant explorer of Chaos
Daring delver in the Eternal
Harry Crosby accepted gallantly the
Only sporting chance life offered
Entered in an uncertain trial heat
By an unknown proprietor
Without even by-your-leave
He vaulted the flimsy fence into
Forbidden fields of Elysium
Sprang out in independent Freedom
Finished the race under his own
Flying colours
Daring to draw down divine wrath

Fearlessly he crashed a
Defiant fist into the
Menacing grinning skull of
That big swaggering bully Existence
He sent hollow Reality reeling
Burst the thin silly shell of
Current Life on this planet
Eager to get at the
Kernel of Creation

Foreseeing possible insufficiency
As an individual atom
Newcome in the Unknown
A half-formed single-sexed
Neophyte in the
Universal Empyrean of Unity
And being born companionate
Humanly he mated in death
To full-form, complete, create
A free future conjugate
For further brilliant adventure
Even ultimate achievement in the
Kaleidoscopic
Blinding black centre of
Seven Trillion Whirling Suns

LA VIE AMERICAINE

8 A.M.	9 A.M.	12 M.
Coffee, cereal cigarettes, eggs	Office $$$$$$$$ chasing the dollar	Brunch

1 P.M.	5 P.M.	7 P.M.
Office $$$$$$£££ dollar-golf chasing	Cocktails	Dinner

8 P.M.		1 A.M.
talkies	chasing the tail	tail-chasing

———————————

&

Yes God
I've looked around
Seen the quaint devices and
Funny commonplaces you bragged about
It's all right God
I understand you're an altruist
Plus God
I know you had a high purpose &
All that God
In breathing your sensen
Semen-scented breath
Into clay pigeons Chinks Brazies
Yanks Frogs Turks and Limeys
It's a great little old world you made God
But now I'm ready for another eyeful
Mars Heaven Hell &/or
What have you got Gott
Come on with your Cummingsesque etceteras

If I
O
Darling
O
Were marooned on a
Little old
Eye of an islette
Dear

I would only
O
Sit
O
Dry-eyed in its center
Scanning the seas
For you
Dear

Fancy in poetry
Now that aeroplanes
Anchor to stars
Is a trifle old-fashioned
Poets who used to yank down
Whole stellar systems to stuff
Their mental mattresses
To-day tug lonelily at their
Inelastic celluloid galluses
Trying to lift by boot-straps
Leaden cloddish earthen poetry feet.
Aeroplanes have made the Muse shy
As Pegasus shied of old on
Encountering unexpected comets

LAMENT OF AN ETCHER

I have etched and etched
Scratched a thousand
Coppers, zincs and alloys
Filled them with criss-crosses
Zig-zags and cross-hatches
Like finely-woven spider-webs
I might have spent my time
To more purpose
Weaving panama hats
For all the public cares
About real Art
And now
Old and broken
Unappreciated
In spite of my exhausting effort
To make the Brooklyn Bridge
Look true to life
As accurate as a photograph
With every cable stretched taut and
All the finely scratched little lines
Just as God put them in our thumbs
I face failure and renounce
The unappreciative public
In future I will devote myself to
An even subtler Art
From this day onward
I will scratch my back
For my own exclusive selfish pleasure

Scratch and scratch it
Backwards and forwards
This way and that
With an old yellow-fingered
Chinese ivory back-scratcher
Shaped as a long-nailed
Grasping ghostly hand
With all my skill
I will scratch
As finely as the finest etching
Grave with supreme technique
Superb sworling compositions
On my back where even I
Cannot see my masterpieces
My art shall henceforth be
Concealed from all
Art for Art's sake

A GRACE BEFORE WRITING

Lord God we have in common
This good language
To nourish us
Lord God keep us
From stammering it
Sipping it
Stuttering it
Snuffling it
Dribbling it on our
Pouter-pigeon breasts
A letter at a time
Like gruelish alphabet soup

WRITING

Apathy of life
Immobility of mind
Sat-on souls
God — on your dump-heap
Throne of punctured tyres
Off Pegasus
Sitting there stolidly
Straight through eternity
Flattening piled tins of
Sardined souls
God — do you never feel like
Getting up to stretch and yawn
Say in the seventh heaven
Just to give the soul-boys
An occasional inning

The snatch of life
Belonging most to me
Is an embroidered, mind-woven strip of being
Fringed along one side by
Lace of dreams
The other edge bound tightly by a
Creamy Chinese silk-band of awakening.
On this strip I sit cross-legged
Weaving the fabric as a caterpillar spins its cocoon
Using threads of experience and imagination in
                                    undreamed design.
I put into it all the unborn butterfly stuff I have
In that small space I am a conscious chrysalid
Neither crawling nor flying
Weaving motifs of the spirit into a colorful scheme
    upon which psychic soul-surges play throbbing
    melodies that elude me when I wake.

    My fabric is a heavenly warp, a field of
        daisies sparkling with little naked girls
        carrying mushroom umbrellas.
    The feel of my giant fingers in the fairy
        web gives me the thrill of creation
    I embroider loud laughs playing leap-frog
        with sneezes, pile up a tempting red-
        ripe mountain of kisses before a pale
        yellow sterile womb that looks like a
        deflated balloon

Picking out any thread I watch it run through the whole living web like fire, diving with sizzling sounds into purple ponds filled with analine green pollywogs which it strings as Brazilian bugs on its golden self and hangs as a necklace over the gleaming burnished ebony breast of a negress who comes up from the center of the pool with laughing lips and redeeming white flashing teeth

Sometimes I lie soft as down on my silken magic carpet and press a button which gives me a pleasant physical thrill and puts me instantly in touch with all humanity

We rub hands, noses, all extremities, including thoughts, and float warmly down a rich river exquisitely perfumed with essence of life, waving to Noah's arks of animals trooping along on the banks, like children bound for a circus

I have seen blacksmiths
Blowing and bellowing
Paper-hangers slapping on glue
Con-men running away
With policemen puffing in pursuit
But for years I have
Peered through venetian blinds
At poets
Without yet catching a glimpse of
One at work

I thought
Anthony Trollope
Had polished off the
Three volume novel
Forever
When along came
Anthony Galsworthy

In the reading-machine future
Say by 1950
All magnum opuses
Will be etched on the
Heads of pins
Not retched into
Three volume classics
By pin heads

SONNET
(count the lines)

She was
Bacchus's Bastard Daughter
With a
Dusty cluster of
Wooden nutmegs in her hair
One aventurine eye
A tinsley laugh *ha ha!*
Rings
Fashioned of green gold tooth fillings
And a hollow
Decadent air
Fit mate for a
Mooing ministter's
Legitimate son

Varlet, bring me paper
No! Not that kind
I would write in ink
As red as your hair
Of nights and beddy battles
Dedicated on the first
Lily-white page
To all bloody
Blushing ladies unfair

With a humble bow to culture
The ship's steward
Flung back the door of the
Veneered bookcase in the
Lounge and there
Dressed in Hart Schaffner and Marx
Impeccable business suits appeared
Nine hundred and fifty-six
Reading books
Ready for any tourist, or other American
To browse hungrily among
The ship gave a lurch
The passenger ran for the rail
My God! he cried
Books in America
Frijoles in Mexico
Leaning far out over the sea
He relieved himself
The steward approached
I thought you wanted a book sir?
We have them in the
Natty sixty dollar suitings
For tired business men
There's a lot of stern-jawed
Purposeful Western books
In Stetson hats
Shown in strong silhouette
I thought you wanted to
Read one of our best
Copyright American novels

The traveller blinked at him and
Replied sourly —
No I distinctly asked for an
Ingersoll watch
It's so refreshing just to sit and
Hear one tick

And you
Have pointed your practical finger
At Jack and his beanstalk
Called him silly
Trading cows
For coloured beans
Tell me then
You cow-traders
What do you get for
Your mooing bossies
One half so fanciful and
Soul satisfying
As coloured beans
That stalk to heaven
Coloured beans
That produce giants
You who know beans no better
Than to thrust them
Up your nose

It isn't
Baking bricks
That makes them
So hard
It's telling them
At the start
They can be
Nothing but bricks